D1084615

Australian
BUSH
FOOD

The Five Mile Press

The Five Mile Press Pty. Ltd.
67 Rushdale Street
Knoxfield Victoria 3180 Australia

First published 1994
Text and design this collection copyright
© The Five Mile Press Pty. Ltd.

Designed by Zoë Murphy
Printed in Singapore

National Library of Australia Cataloguing-in-Publication data:
Ross, Joy, 1942-
Australian bush food
ISBN 0 86788 832 6
1. Cookery (Wild foods). 2. Wild foods — Australia.
3. Wild plants, Edible — Australia. I. Title.
641.60994

CONTENTS

— INTRODUCTION —

When the English white settlers came to Australia they brought beef cattle and sheep, and there was no hestitation in killing them for meat. Kangaroos were always in plentiful supply, but it was only the Aborigines who realised their nutritional value.

Following English settlement, the Irish, Europeans and Asians arrived. They, too, brought their home-country recipes with them, so it is little wonder Australia is a country without cooking frontiers. Perhaps that's not such a bad thing after all, as we can enjoy most of the world's cuisine right here in our own backyard.

However, over the years, some white Australians have developed relationships with Aborigines who have shown the vast amount of bush food that Australia has to offer. Most of us have not been aware of our natural plant and animal resources.

Working closely with Aborigines, scientists are educating us about Australia's naturally occurring and nutritious foods. Until recently, few of us knew that the Kakadu plum has the world's highest fruit source of vitamin C and kangaroo meat has one of the lowest cholesterol levels of all red meats.

Perhaps it is time to re-educate our palates. Of course, not all native foods will be to your liking, but on your next holiday, or while still at home, experiment with these basic bush food recipes. Hopefully this book will encourage thoughts about the value of some of Australia's native food.

Camp Oven Cooking

Always make a good fire so there are plenty of coals available to do your cooking with. Mulga wood always gives a good fire with coals that last, but pine, for instance, flares up and burns, then goes to ash leaving few coals.

Cooking The main point to remember is that the oven doesn't need many coals under it, or on the lid, to cook most dishes. First, put the oven on the main fire to heat it up, so that when placed on the coals it already has plenty of heat. When you need heat from above, for foods such as breads, pastries and cakes, get the lid very hot on the fire. Then when you put it on the camp oven it will give immediate heat. If rain falls while you are cooking simply place a piece of tin, or even the blade of a shovel, over the top, otherwise the rain will cool down the oven.

Camp oven care *Never* pour cold water into a hot camp oven. The oven will crack. When washing it, always use hot or warm water. After washing, put a little oil or fat inside and wipe it around. This will prevent your oven from rusting.

Oven Heats by Paper Test

Place a piece of white paper inside the oven to find out what heat the oven has reached:

Heat	Degrees	Paper Test
too hot		black and on fire
very hot oven	500	dark brown
hot oven	375-400	light brown
moderate oven	325-375	yellow
slow oven	250-325	crust

WARNING!

Much native flora is protected and/or toxic. Similarly, most native fauna is protected or needs a valid hunting permit according to each State's regulations.

BARRAMUNDI

Although Australia is often referred to as 'Down Under', especially overseas, we are proud of our Top End. It's here that barramundi love to swim in warm waters. In fact, it can be fished from the northern waters of Queensland across to the north coast of Western Australia.

The name barramundi comes from an Aboriginal language and relates to a fish with large scales. Sometimes known as barramunda or giant perch, it's an edible Australian lungfish with paddle-like fins and a long body. It swims in both fresh and salt waters and has a blue-grey upper body, while its silver sides have a yellowish tinge.

A firm, sweet fish with white flesh, it can be cooked with wild ginger, in paperbark, or simply baked on top of hot coals.

Barramundi in Paperbark

For this recipe, the gum leaves and paperbark are the easiest ingredients to find. Gum trees are prolific in Australia and the well-known Melaleuca tree has papery bark.

Native limes are usually found in dry rainforests or arid areas and are fruits of several varieties of indigenous citrus.

- 1 barramundi
- 2 native limes (optional)
- gum leaves
- paperbark

Method: Scale and gut the barramundi, and rinse well. Rub limes over the fish. Dampen paperbark, place a thin layer of gum leaves between fish and bark, and wrap barramundi completely in the bark, ensuring that the paperbark covers the fish.

Move some fire coals away and dig a hole under the fire about 30 cm deep. Put a layer of coals in bottom, place fish on coals then cover with remaining

Barramundi

coals. Seal coals with sand or dirt and leave for about one to one and a half hours. This cooking time depends on size of fish.

Whole Barramundi in Coals

- 1 whole barramundi, gutted
- bed of hot coals
- paperbark or banana leaf plates
- gum leaves for resting fish

Method: The scales are left on this whole barramundi to protect its tasty flesh. It also makes turning easier. Place gutted barramundi on top of very hot coals. To avoid any burning, turn fish frequently. Cooking time depends on size of fish and heat of coals. Cooked flesh is white.

When cooked, remove from fire and place on gum leaves or available fresh leaves. Insert knife along backbone, halve and remove the bones. Remember to eat the cheek, as this is a 'prime cut.'

BEEF

Whilst beef cattle are not native to Australia, beef steaks are still thought of as traditional Aussie bush tucker.

Beef is rich red in colour, with marbled streaks of fat which increase the tenderness and juiciness of the cooked meat. Aussies travelling in the bush for long periods of time, sometimes take canned, cured, smoked or dried beef. But for the tired drover, a thick loin or porterhouse steak or Aussie burgers pan fried or cooked on coals, is a day's filling reward.

Hot Coal Steaks with Native Peppercorns

- *steak for each person*
- *a few small branches of native peppercorns*

Method: When energy is somewhat depleted after a hard day in the bush, a camp fire is a must. To throw peppercorn branches and steaks on to hot coals takes very little energy and certainly revives strength.

Shovel Aussie burgers

These days, bush rovers are usually well equipped with utensils, but a shovel has many uses and one can be that of a grill plate.

- *a quantity of finely chopped beef*
- *½ pannikin (cup) flour*
- *½ pannikin soaked damper crumbs*
- *1 egg*
- *a sprinkling of dried onion flakes*
- *lard*

Method: Simply mix all ingredients and form into hamburger shapes. Over hot coals, heat lard on hot plate/shovel and fry burgers. A fun experiment with a tasty result.

Boab fruit

— BOAB TREE —

The shape of a boab has many similarities to a young child's drawing of a tree. It has a round, thick and straight trunk with hollows that trap water. The tree is stout rather than tall. Branches are similar in shape, but not as thick.

The round, gourd-like fruit has many seeds buried in its edible and meaty pulp. The seeds can be eaten fresh or roasted separately and served like peanuts. They can also be used for sprouting.

After eating a substantial meal from the boab's abundant crop, Aborigines made a drink by mixing boab tree sap with water.

Roasted Boab Fruit and Seeds

* *immature boab fruit (greenish rather than brown, on gourd-like skin)*

Method: Place fruit on warm coals (if the coals are too hot, the fruit may explode) and gently roast.

When broken in half, the warm pulp is similar to stewed fruit.

Boab seeds can also be roasted in a wooden coolamon or dish. A coolamon is made from wood or bark and is primarily used by Aborigines to carry water. Simply place warm coals and boab seeds in coolamon and toss until cooked.

— BOGONG MOTHS —

When flying either on business or pleasure these days, don't be surprised if you come across Bogong moth toast. Bogong moths are being ground into spreads, powdered as an ingredient for damper, as well as being roasted and served as a nut substitute with beer.

If you were blind-folded and someone popped one of these roasted insects into your mouth (without you knowing what it was) you would think that you were eating a peanut. Such is the likeness.

Aboriginal groups in the Australian alps of New South Wales and across a large area of Victoria, saw Bogong moths as tasty and nutritious, and one of their staple foods. During summer, moths congregated in rock caverns and it was then that the Aborigines collected and feasted on them. Bogong moths tossed in a wooden coolamon of hot coals are most enjoyable.

Coolamon Moth Nuts

- 1 coolamon
- a quantity of Bogong moths

Method: In Australia there are often plagues of Bogong moths. When this happens, moths can be caught, cleaned and frozen for future cooking. If a coolamon is not available, moths can be placed in a pan or appropriate dish.

From a fire, place several live coals on top of a coolamon of moths. Gently mix and when the coals cool, replace with hot coals. Continue in this way until the moths have been warmed and debris rubs off. When cooked, the moths' nutty and oily flavours are enhanced.

— AUSSIE BREAD —

Damper is the bush bread of Australia. It is usually thought of as unleavened bread cooked on an open fire. Today, self-raising often replaces plain flour, powdered milk replaces water and butter is added.

The best part about cooking damper or bread in the bush, is that as long as you allow it to rise, your ingredients can vary and they don't have to be precisely measured. You can wander around the bush and find something that you can add. Native peppercorns, lemon myrtle leaves, Macadamia nuts or pulped Bogong moths are just a few.

Modern Damper

- *2 pannikins (cups) self-raising flour*
- *½ teaspoon salt*
- *1 pannikin milk*
- *1 tablespoon butter*

Method: Sift flour and salt and rub in butter. Mix in enough milk to make a non-sticky dough. Allow it to sit while sides and bottom of camp oven are floured.

Put camp oven on hot coals and place dough in oven. Cook for about half an hour. Damper is cooked when it is golden brown and when tapped, it sounds hollow inside.

Aussie Beer Bread

- 3 pannikins (cups) self-raising flour
- ½ pannikin sugar
- 1 pinch salt
- 1 can beer

Method: The beer is the secret ingredient and replaces any yeast used. Make sure that your hot coals have settled and have your camp oven ready. Mix all ingredients together, forming a semi-dry dough, and place in floured camp oven. Cook for 30-40 minutes. When cooked, take a clean leaf, paint butter over bread, pull apart and start eating!

BUFFALO

For many years large numbers of water buffaloes roamed throughout the Northern Territory, but it is only recently that they have been introduced as a table meat. Farmed buffalo meat is now in demand both locally and internationally.

Older water buffaloes have a 'darker than beef' coloured meat, whilst the younger meat is a lighter pink. Primal cuts are offered: steaks are very popular, but it's generally considered that the eye fillet is the most tender. These fillets are similar in size to beef.

The water buffalo's name came from the fact that these animals love to soak in water for hours at a time. Water buffaloes also produce milk.

Rough Red Buffalo Steaks

- *1 × 2.5 cm buffalo steak, per person — 2.5 cm thick*
- *some rough red wine*

Sliced buffalo

- *local native herbs*
- *animal fat or oil*

Method: It's good to marinate buffalo overnight. Cover steaks with red wine, chopped local herbs and some oil if you have it. Turn a few times during the marination.

An hour or so before eating, prepare a fire. When coals are hot, heat pan by hanging over coals and then melt fat or oil before cooking. Place steaks in pan and grill for a few minutes before turning. Add a little of the marinade to the pan.

Grill for about five minutes before turning again and repeating the process. At this stage the buffalo steaks should be medium rare.

Serve steaks on tin plates. To add to the richness of flavour, quickly reduce any leftover marinade and pour over buffalo. Enjoy this taste sensation with local mint or herb tea.

— BUNYA BUNYA NUT —

Scientific studies show that Queensland's bunya bunya nut has no fat at all. In addition, because of its slow-releasing carbohydrate properties, it is an excellent food for diabetics.

Bunya bunya nuts come from the large rainforest tree known as bunya pine. It is similar in looks to the hoop and Norfolk Island pine. During autumn, bunya trees drop huge cones full of seeds. The seeds or nuts taste like young waxy potatoes and are very filling. Aborigines saw them as an important food source. Next time you are roving around the mountains of southern Queensland or their nearby parks, keep a look out for fallen bunya bunya nuts. The trees are so tall, that steps are sometimes cut into the trunks to allow climbing to the nut-bearing cones.

Bunya bunya nuts can be used in a variety of ways: soups, pies desserts and sweets.

Bunya Toffee

When you're out in the bush you can often feel like something sweet like toffee. This is a fairly basic recipe, but great!

- 2 pannikins (cups) bunya bunya nuts
- 1½ pannikins sugar
- ¼ pannikin glucose syrup or Aussie golden syrup
- ½ pannikin water

Method: In a heavy-duty saucepan over fire, boil the bunya nuts. Cool, peel shells and cut in half. Place halved nuts on greased hot plate.

Combine sugar, syrup and water in saucepan over coals and stir without boiling until sugar is dissolved. Boil, without stirring, for about 10 minutes, until mixture thickens. Take off heat and pour over nuts. Cool. When set, break toffee and nut-chew contentedly.

Bush tomato

BUSH TOMATO

With increased demands for bush tucker, it is great when bush foods regenerate quickly. Bush tomatoes, an Australian relative of both the tomato and potato, with a tamarillo-like flavour, do just that.

A lot of bush tomatoes are found and harvested in central Australia. When you fly over the area, you can see where bulldozers have cut up areas for road making. It is along these diggings you can also see young, regenerating bush tomato plants.

Marble-sized bush tomatoes are also known as desert raisins, because in the hot central Australian sun, they sometimes shrivel on the shrub and look like raisins.

For bush-cooking they make a good sauce and are a great additive to a tin of tomato soup or tinned tomatoes.

Desert Tomato Soup

- *1 large tin of tomatoes or tomato soup*
- *½–1 pannikin (cup) bush tomatoes*
- *native peppercorns and salt*
- *local herbs*
- *1 pannikin water*
- *vegetable stock cube, optional*

Method: In a camp oven over hot coals, add tinned tomatoes and mash them with a fork. (If you are using tomato soup, increase the amount of water.) Add finely chopped bush tomatoes, seasonings, herbs, crumbled stock cube and water. Simmer for at least half an hour, until the soup thickens. Cooking time depends a lot on the heat of coals. A great drink or meal around the camp fire.

CROCODILE

Aborigines knew large crocodiles were not difficult to catch at any time, but after big floods, crocodiles were often stranded in small water-holes and could be speared easily.

Salt-water crocodiles were not always hunted by Aborigines for food. Those who did, prized the tail for its fat and flavour, and ground the backbone for important minerals like phosphorous and calcium. These minerals balanced their basically dairy-free diet.

Today, both freshwater and salt-water crocodiles are farmed in pens until they are about two metres long. They are then culled.

A crocodile steak is virtually fat free and has a centre bone. When char-grilled it has a similar colour and flavour to pork, but a texture not unlike tuna.

Crocodile steaks

Slightly Gum-smoked Crocodile

Other ingredients used in this recipe include native peppers which have branches of small pinky-red fruit. Their seeds can be ground into pepper, while lemon aspen is found in the rainforests of the eastern coast of Australia. It is a small yellow fruit with a citrus tang, and is often used to replace lemon juice. In contrast, the native lime grows in drier areas.

- *1 crocodile steak per person*
- *freshly ground peppercorns*
- *lemon aspen or lime juice to cover steaks*
- *gum or tea tree branches*

Method: Over a bed of hot coals, simply place grill or pan over gum or tea tree branches. Rub crocodile steaks with juice and sprinkle with pepper. Put on grill or in pan and turn a couple of times until the steaks are medium rare.

EMU

Australia must be one of the few countries that commercially exports both elements of its emblem; the kangaroo and emu. The emu is a large Australian flightless bird, with an ostrich-like body and dark plumage. Within the country, emus are sometimes considered pests, because they eat crops and break down fences. However, it was the Western Australian government who first allowed emu farming by the Aborigines. Farmed birds and fertilized eggs were then sold to Western Australian farmers.

Today, much of the commercial farming and processing of the birds is conducted in the state of Western Australia. By selectively cross-breeding birds from the west, other states are now farming in smaller quantities, although emu meat regulations still vary from state to state.

The emu's lean red meat is classed as poultry and is light in protein and iron. It's flavour is gamey, yet exudes a sweet aftertaste. A hind-quarter of emu can be roasted or sliced into steaks. Fillets of emu cooked on a grill over hot coals, are certainly worth tasting.

Emu meat is still reasonably expensive, so smoked or char-grilled slithers of emu are popular. Emu slithers are exported to countries such as France, U.S.A. and Japan.

Other products used from the emu include eggs which also have a strong game flavour. One emu egg is equal to about seven hen eggs. The emu's hide is tanned commercially and its fat is made into emu oil.

Barbecued Emu

• *1 young emu hen*

Method: Place emu on coals in a good-sized hole, and cover with gum or green branches. Cook until the feathers have disappeared and skin is golden brown.

Rub with mallee (green) roots to remove the quills. Serve on tin plates: a real Aussie bushfood delicacy.

KANGAROO

Some people still think that Australians ride kangaroos. This is certainly not the case. Kangaroos are relatively lean in build and are continually hopping, so it would be almost impossible to sit on one, let alone stay on one.

They are a much loved national symbol and everyone enjoys seeing them either in the wild or in animal parks. Their fur has been sold commercially for some time, but kangaroo meat has only recently been marketed nationally and internationally. Aborigines however, have been eating kangaroo meat for centuries.

Kangaroos were hunted by being stalked, speared from hiding-areas, trapped by fire or driven into traps. Some stories tell of kangaroos being chased until they dropped. One can only postulate about the energy and perseverence of Aborigines!

South Australia was the first state to establish a legal processing plant for kangaroo meat intended for the table. Other states are slowly recognizing the value of this animal product. Kangaroo hindquarter cuts include saddle, porterhouse steak, fillet, tail and minced meat.

Experts advise to cook kangaroo meat slowly. It's flesh is dark red in colour and has one of the lowest cholesterol levels of all red meats. Kangaroo meat texture is not unlike that of beef; its flavour a little stronger. Many Australian bushmen carry sufficient provisions to cook kangaroo in a variety of ways; kangaroo tail soup; braised kangaroo tail; roasted leg of kangaroo; kangaroo rissoles; kangaroo stew or barbecued fillet.

Kangaroo Tail Soup

This recipe should be started early in the day. Cooking time is about three hours, so there's plenty of time to enjoy the pleasures of the bush between the preparing and eventually sipping of the soup.

- *6 joints of kangaroo tail*
- *water*

- 1 cup split peas
- 2 onions
- dried noodles, macaroni or spaghetti
- any vegetables you may have, fresh, tinned or dried
- salt and pepper to taste

Method: Heat empty camp oven on a bed of coals and then add jointed kangaroo tail.

Cover with the water and bring to the boil. Add the split peas, onions and dried noodles, macaroni or spaghetti to the boiling water. Boil until all is cooked, including the meat. Add the vegetables you have diced. Cook until these are tender, then add the salt and pepper. Serves 6-8.

Roasted Kangaroo Leg

This recipe came from the famous Australian outback painter and cook, Jack Absalom. He relates that he has served this bushfood meal to governors, millionaires, television crews and hundreds of people and never had a complaint. Cooking time: 2½–3 hours.

Kangaroo roast

Kangaroo rissoles

- 1 kangaroo leg
- 1 cup dripping

Stuffing
- ½ loaf bread
- 1 large onion, *chopped finely*
- 2 strips bacon, *chopped finely*
- 2 soft tomatoes, *chopped finely*
- 1 dessertspoon mixed herbs
- 1 egg
- salt and pepper to taste

Method: Take the kangaroo leg and cut pockets well into the leg to hold the stuffing once it is pushed in. To make the stuffing cut the crust off the bread and crumb it. Add the bacon, onion and tomatoes. Rub well together with the breadcrumbs then add the egg, mix well, adding herbs then salt and pepper and stuff this into pockets of the kangaroo leg. Bake in camp oven with the cup of dripping until well cooked — about 2½-3 hours. Remember to baste the meat all the time because it has no fat.

Kangaroo Rissoles

This recipe calls for a bushman's pack having the staple provision of onions, potatoes, egg and the Australian favourite sauce, tomato.

- *1 kg kangaroo meat*
- *2 onions*
- *2 potatoes*
- *1 egg*
- *tomato sauce*
- *salt and pepper*

Method: Cut up small, or mince the meat with the onions and potatoes. Add the salt and pepper, mix together then add the egg for binding. Make into balls and place in camp oven. Place a dessertspoon of tomato sauce on each ball and bake slowly.

LILLYPILLY

The lillypilly *(Eugenia smithii)* is just one of many Australian native lillypillies grown as street trees and planted in gardens from Victoria to Queensland.

It's sometimes hard to pick these edible white, lilac or purple berries, because of the height of the trees. However, lillypilly fruit is rather prolific and many fall to the ground and, as long as they are not bruised, can be used for jellies, glazes, tarts, vinegar or as an accompaniment to fish and meat.

Lillypillies have a watermelon texture, but they vary from sour to a strong cinnamon and clove-like taste. When preserved, their flavour is less pungent. Interestingly, the Victorian lillypilly is good for making vinegar, whilst on the far north coast of New South Wales, lillypillies are too strong to use by themselves. Their fruit is made into jams, chutneys and jellies, or used in a sauce on red or white meat.

Lillypilly

If you are in the bush and have lillypillies galore and a few hours to spare, a lillypilly vinegar is an easy accompaniment to go with the catch of the day.

Easy Lillypilly Vinegar

- 2kg lillypillies, *plain or mixed including magenta variety*
- 3 litres white wine vinegar
- 1 camp oven

Method: These quantities are a guide and can be reduced or increased dependent upon your lillypilly quantities. Place camp oven on hot coals, add vinegar and fruit. Simmer for about two hours. Cool slightly and strain through muslin cloth or whatever is available in the bush.

Any leftover, oriental spice-flavoured vinegar can be placed in an empty bottle, ready for your next food catch.

— MACADAMIA NUTS —

Macadamia nuts are Australia's first commercially-grown native food. They were named after the scientist John MacAdam, who studied the nuts' nutritional content. Both Aborigines and early settlers saw the nut as an excellent food source. The nuts' fat content is about 70%, but most of this is mono-saturated fat. They also have a very high energy, protein content.

In Queensland, macadamia trees grow to a height of about 20 metres. Although a large tree, it can be grown in domestic gardens, not just for the nut, but also for creating a block-out of a neighbouring view.

Macadamias can take up to five years to produce fruit, but can be quite prolific once they start. Nuts appear six to nine months after flowering. The nut case is hard to break, even when the husk is removed. Like a lot of native food, the less done to it the better. Macadamia nuts are delightful when eaten raw or simply roasted in a camp fire. However for cooking, these nuts are such a versatile ingredient they can be used in butters, oils, jams, vegetables, fruit salads, breads and ice creams.

Macadamia Pop

Instead of going to the picture theatre to eat your popcorn, it's much nicer to sit around a camp fire and have your camp oven popping moths and roasting madacamias.

- *Some macadamia nut oil*
- *a handful of macadamia nuts, husks with cases removed*
- *a handful of Bogong moths, optional*

Method: Put camp oven on hot coals, heat macadamia oil and add nuts and moths. Shake them around the oven until roasted. The moths will dry and taste like peanuts. The macadamia nuts will be sensational.

Macadamia nuts

MARRON

An Australian freshwater crayfish, marron are most plentiful in south-west Western Australia, where they are farmed for national and international gourmet eating.

Queensland waters also have a slightly different native marron known as redclaw. Both varieties are similar to yabbies, but the marron has five ridges on the back of its head. A pair of centre spines on the tail fan is another distinguishing feature.

Whilst the catching of marron was once confined to the large and permanent freshwater pools of coastal streams, they have now been introduced to man-made water systems. Unlike other native species, they have difficulty surviving when these ponds dry up in summer.

Their reddish shell, which in the first couple of years may shed many times, is hidden in daylight hours and emerges at sunset. If you are camping near a freshwater pool, you can coax marron by feeding them with a piece of fish or meat on a line and then netting them by hand. Always have your hot coals and camp oven ready so that you can quickly boil, shell and devour these nibbles.

Marron Bush-Gourmet Nibbles

- marrons, as many as required per person
- water
- white wine, if available
- native peppercorns
- salt

Method: In a camp oven resting on hot coals, bring water to the boil. Add wine, peppercorns, salt and finally, the marrons. Simmer for about two minutes. At this stage they will have bright red shells. Dunk marrons in cold water. When coolish, twist the body from the head and nibble away at this delicately flavoured morsel.

MULLET

The sea mullet is probably Australia's most common edible food. With its camouflaged olive-green top and silvery sides, it is prolific in all states except Tasmania. An average-sized fish is about 1 kg and 45 cm long. The flesh is excellent and is often smoked, fried or grilled.

On the other hand, the flat-tail mullet which is also known as jumping mullet (it actually jumps up in the water) is very common in estuaries around Australia, again with the exception of Tasmania. The flat-tail mullet is light brown with a silvery underbelly and about 30 cm long. Its flesh is oily and fish lovers either like or dislike the flavour.

Mullet in Banana Leaves over Coals

Because bananas are prevalent from northern New South Wales right into Queensland, wanderers will have a good chance of finding banana leaves in that area. Paperbark is a good alternative.

- 2 average-sized mullet
- 1 native lime or lemon
- native peppercorns and salt, to taste
- banana leaves

Method: Quickly dunk banana leaves in boiling water, cool and trim. Scale and clean mullet. Place a few shallow slashes across the mullet and insert slithers of lime or lemon. Put remaining citrus in fish cavity. Rub fish with a little salt and place a few peppercorns or leaves around fish.

Lay mullet on individual banana leaves, sprinkle with a little water and wrap. Tie firmly with banana leaf strips. Place in warm coals and cook for about 30-40 minutes. Open leaves toward the end of cooking. When ready to serve the skin will lift easily and the flesh will flake. If you have any leftover banana leaves, place charred leaf and cooked fish on a fresh banana leaf plate.

MUNTHARIES

Throughout the year, Aborigines had a wonderful choice of hundreds of different fruits and berries. Popular along the South Australian sand dune area was, and still is. the munthari. This small, apple-flavoured furry berry, also known as an emu apple and as native cranberry, has a subtle crab apple flavour.

The munthari is a ground cover creeper with white spiky blossom in spring and early summer. When muntharies are producing their pea-sized fruit, you are attracted to the pleasant, apple-smelling sand dunes.

You, too, can be like the Aborigines who lived by the sea and enjoyed the best of both worlds. They combined whatever seafood and bush fruits were available at the time. Muntharies can be eaten fresh, used in fruit pies or as sauces.

Native Munthari Sauce

- *muntharies*
- *¼ pannikin oil*
- *3 drops edible eucalyptus oil*
- *2 lemon myrtle or lemon flavoured herbs*
- *salt*
- *2 tbsp butter, optional*

Method: If you are cooking meat or fish prior to making the sauce, just use the remaining pan liquid to make the sauce. Place pan on camp fire. Mix the two oils and add butter and the oil mixture to pan. Now add muntharies, lemon myrtle leaves or herbs and toss until reduced and cooked. A creative bush flavoured sauce.

Munthari

Murray River cray

MURRAY RIVER CRAYFISH

In Australia, crayfish and lobster are names both used to describe the sea crayfish, like the rock lobster, which are caught in Australian waters. The freshwater species of crayfish include marron, yabbies and the Murray River crayfish.

If you are roaming around the Murray and Murrumbidgee rivers of New South Wales and Victoria and the streams are clear, you could see some Murray crays. They are about 30 cm in length and can be up to one kilogram in weight. The Murray River variety has an unusual blue-black body with cream claws. Body and claws are white-tipped.

If you throw in a line with a fish or meat bait, you might be able to coax them up and into your landing net. It's best to kill these crustaceans just before cooking. This ensures not only freshness, but an excellent flavour and texture. If you see one, it's wise to test your fishing skills. Your reward will be delectable.

Char-Grilled Crayfish

- *1 fresh Murray River crayfish*
- *½ pannikin (cup) oil (butter is better but melts in backpacks!)*
- *½ pannikin native lime or lemon juice*
- *native peppercorns and salt*

Method: Heat grill over hot coals. Break lobster in half and split tail down the centre. Mix ingredients thoroughly. Baste crayfish with mix and place shell side down on grill. Cook four minutes, turn and cook meat side for two minutes. Baste again and repeat the procedure for about 15-20 minutes.

When cooked, crayfish meat is white and mouthwatering.

MUSSEL

The Victorian coastline and much of the state of Tasmania have mussels: these bi-value shellfish are found in inlets and bays south of about 30° latitude.

Before preparing them for a meal, make sure that they are fresh. The shells should be closed; if they are only slightly open, tap them with your finger and if they close straight away, use them. Discard those that don't close. It's important to carefully wash the mussel and remove its fibrous, clinging beard.

The easiest way to open the mussels is to barbecue or steam them in a camp oven with water, or a little white wine and herbs. Don't put too many mussels in the oven; allow room for mussels to open. Put lid on camp oven and simmer for a couple of minutes.

Even in the bush, you can serve mussels in many ways; they make a particularly easy hors d'oeuvre when they are wrapped in bacon and quickly heated over hot coals.

Mussels, Rice and (Bush) Tomatoes

- *20 mussels or as many as you like, beards removed*
- *10 ripe bush tomatoes or prepared tomato chutney*
- *3 cups cooked rice*
- *local herbs*

Method: Place heavy duty saucepan over hot coals. Heat four cups of salted water and boil rice. While cooking, prepare tomatoes and mussels.

Bush tomatoes are more inclined to be found a little further north than where mussels are found, however, a heated chutney with a few herbs, mixed through, makes a great topping. If you do have tomatoes, chop and simmer them in some water or wine and herbs until they reduce and thicken. Place camp oven over hot coals. Add water or wine and herbs to the oven and steam clean mussels for a few minutes. Top rice with drained mussels in their shells and pour thickened tomatoes over. Appetizing tucker.

– PLUMS AND ROSELLA – FLOWER

The Davidson, Illawarra and Kakadu plums are now being widely used in bush food cuisine. A delightful Australian bush jam is made from the soft, juicy pulp of the Davidson plum. It also makes a very popular sauce or glaze. The tree grows in the rainforests of New South Wales and Queensland.

The Illawarra purple/brown plum, also known as brown pine plum, has an external seed and the edible area is the larger, swollen stem. It grows well in the rainforests along Australia's eastern coast and can be used in sauces, jams and tarts. The fruit is slightly bitter and should not be tasted when hot. The bitterness lessens when cool.

The most nutritious of the native plums is the Kakadu plum, found within a far northern Australian area of the same name in the Northern Territory. The Kakadu plum contains the world's highest fruit source of vitamin C, and is harvested in both tropical and desert regions. The fruit can be picked, stewed or included in soups such as kangaroo tail.

The native rosella is not only a species of parrot, but a small tree or shrub (Hibiscus heterophyllus) found in the damp forest areas of eastern Australia. Its yellow or white flowers can be eaten raw, mixed in salads or used in chutney. Rosella buds make excellent jam, with a flavour comparable to a plum. The native rosella is a very useful vegetable; its leaves taste like sorrel and can be used in pastry or as a herb. The flavour of its roots is not unlike that of parsnip.

PRAWNS

'Don't come the raw prawn with me,' is Australian slang; roughly meaning, 'Don't pretend when you do know something, that you don't,' or 'Don't pretend to be green.' Interestingly, raw prawns, whatever their colour, are known as 'green prawns'. Exo-skeletal raw prawns come in various shapes as well as colours.

Most prawns are found in the warmer, northern waters of Australia. The cream-yellow banana male prawn is about 42 mm long, whilst its female counterpart's length is about 45 mm.

Banana prawns are netted in deep waters such as the Gulf of Carpentaria. They are also seen further south in Nickol Bay, Western Australia. The popular eastern king prawn is found from Lakes Entrance in Victoria and northwards along Australia's eastern coast to the North Reef in Queensland. They are caught during spring and summer in estuaries. The way to attract prawns is to wade in some of these shallow waters with a hand-held net and a bright light. Like most shellfish, the simplest cooking preparation usually ends up with the best results. Flavours are so delicate that any heavy ingredients served with prawns tend to be too dominant.

Grilled Prawns with Native Citrus

- green prawns, as many as you can eat
- lemon aspen fruit, lemon myrtle or lemon-scented tea tree leaves, native limes or lemons

Method: Whole prawns can be just thrown on a greased cast iron plate which is sitting in hot coals. Baste with citrus juice, or add citrus leaves to the cooking plate. The flavour will permeate into the prawns. If you are fussy in the bush and want to shell the prawns before cooking, always remember to remove the dark tract which runs down the back of the tail. There is another benefit in shelling your prawns; you can make soup stock with the shells.

QUANDONG

The quandong, or native peach, is found in the arid areas of southern Australia. It has a sweet, yet slightly acidic flavour and is rich in vitamin C. Early colonists used the seeds inside the fruit to make artifacts like beads, buttons and game tokens. The fruit's kernel can be eaten fresh or roasted.

The tree prospers well in both semi-arid and better-watered areas and this feature alone is of a particular advantage, when other trees will not grow. The quandong's red fruit is used for jams, jellies and as a stewed fruit.

Stewed Quandongs

- *quandongs*
- *sugar to sweeten slightly*
- *water*

A rough idea of fruit/sugar ratio is about 1 panni-kin (cup) of sugar to 400gms of pitted fresh fruit.

Method: Put heavy-duty saucepan over hot coals, add fruit and sugar and sufficient water to cover both. Gently simmer quandongs until soft. At this stage the fruit will be slightly acidic and have a plum/peach texture. Enjoy quandongs in their delicately flavoured juices or, for extra flavour and texture, mix in some chopped macadamia nuts.

Quandong

Riberry

RIBERRY

Riberries or small-leafed, clove lillypilly fruit are often used in fruit tarts. Some riberries have seeds, others don't: the seedless are preferred. If you come across riberries whilst walking in the bush, pick some and make a sauce to accompany your evening meal.

Riberry Sauce

- *riberries*
- *meat or vegetable stock*
- *water*

Method: After cooking your camp oven meal, remove it from the camp oven but reserve any stock. Add a little water, crush the riberries and add to oven. Reduce liquid and soften fruit. At this stage the liquid is like a shiny glaze. Serve as a nutritious sauce with your main meal.

SALMON

Whilst not native to Australia, the gourmet Atlantic salmon was, some time ago, introduced into the lakes, rivers and dams of New South Wales with limited success.

However, in the 1980s Atlantic salmon farming commenced in southern Tasmania and today it's a thriving business. Tasmanian Atlantic salmon is now regarded as an Australian food delight and if you are wandering in southern Tasmania, it's worth a look at the salmon farms.

With pinkish-apricot flesh, the salmon's flavour is delicate and distinctive.

Salmon over coals

- *1 salmon, gutted and cut into cutlets*
- *oil*

Method: Whilst salmon is an oily fish, when placed on a grill over coals, or even in a pan, it dries very quickly. Brush salmon cutlets with oil and place on char-grill over coals. Cook for about four minutes on either side — of course this depends on the thickness of the cutlet and the heat of the coals. Eat immediately.

Poached Camp Salmon

- *one 3 kg whole salmon*
- *a camp oven or poacher, with rack*
- *native peppercorn leaves*

Method: The oven or poacher must be sitting in a good sized fire of hot coals and ashes. Fill the container with about 3 cm of water and bring to boil. Put rack over water and position the fish. Be careful that the gently boiling water doesn't boil dry and poach for about one hour. Garnish your salmon with native peppercorn leaves.

Tasmanian Atlantic Salmon

— SYDNEY'S SEAFOOD —

Sydney's prolific rock oysters have an international reputation for their flavour. They are smaller than many varieties, and able to survive in their shell, but out of water, for a couple of weeks. Cultivation of the Sydney rock oyster is not limited to New South Wales. In fact, you can take oysters from the rocks at Tin Can Bay in Queensland, south through to Victoria's Mallacoota Inlet.

However, the laws governing these oysters allow you to eat as many as you can, where you find them, but don't tolerate you taking them home or back to your camp fire.

In these same waterways and further south to Tasmania and South Australia, pipis, in their wedged-shaped shells, live intertidally, just a few centimetres below the sandy beaches. These tasty delights are among the native shellfish and seafoods that are exciting both local and overseas palates. Sydney's

Balmain bugs are regarded as a flat marine lobster and very much like Queensland's Moreton Bay lobster. If you are able to net some, you will have a hearty feed.

Crabs are also plentiful and an excellent food source. The stunningly-coloured blue swimmers are usually caught in cone-shaped traps. They die within hours of being caught, so it is wise to catch and cook them straight away.

Rock Oysters

International chefs often suggest that the best way to eat oysters is to serve them cleaned and raw, sprinkled only with lemon juice and ground pepper. A fantastic, yet simple meal for campers.

Sydney Beaches Pipi Soup

Pipis are found in beach sands between high and low tide levels. They are members of the cockle family. Pipi gourmands often simply clean the pipis, cover them in lemon or native lime juice and roll them up in damper.

- About 20 pipis
- 300 mls milk
- seasoned flour
- native herbs

Method: Soak the pipis in water for about two hours. This will remove the sand. Place camp oven on hot coals with about 1 cm of water, add pipis and when shells open, add 600 mls of water and simmer for about 10 minutes. Strain and add the milk. Thicken with the seasoned flour blended with a little of the milk. Serve and sprinkle with native herbs.

Blue Swimmers and Beer

- blue swimmer crabs per person
- salt

Method: Blue swimmer crabs need to be soaked for an hour or so in water. When ready to cook, boil lots of water in camp oven, add salt and crabs and boil for 15 minutes. Cool.

Some bush folk say that it's sacrilege to serve crabs with vegetables or salad greens. They insist you cut the body lengthways and remove the meat with a sharp and pointed knife. Crack the claws and legs with a hammer and serve meat with a can of cold beer!

TROUT

An introduced species, today trout is commonplace around Australia. Commercial hatcheries breed trout and state governments release trout into public waters. The popular rainbow and brown trout are prolific in Australia's cooler, southern waters. Brown trout becomes a more dominant species when it shares water with a rainbow trout. Ocean trout is now being farmed successfully in Tasmania.

Coral trout are widely dispersed around the coral reef waters of Queensland, the Northern Territory and Western Australia. They have small blue spots over their body and head, and range in colour from pink to reddish-brown. Coral trout can weigh up to 20 kgs and when cooked, their white flesh is delicious.

If you wake up early and are camped by a mountain stream, trout makes a wonderful pan-fried breakfast. It's important not to over-cook trout, because the delicate flavour will be lost and the fish will be too dry to really enjoy.

Trout in the Mud

- *1 large trout*
- *mud or clay to cover fish*

Method: Place some newspaper on the ground and shape a mud or clay mould around the fish. Mud thickness should be about 1.5 cm. (When wrapping meat in mud or clay, it should be a little thicker.)

Dig a hollow in the coals, add the mud-coated fish and cover with coals and ashes. Cook for about 45 minutes, remove mud-fish and cool the casing until you can smash it. The skin and scales will come away from the fish and you will be left with a beautifully moist trout. Remove the small lump inside the fish. This is the gut. Serve while still fairly hot.

Rainbow Trout

Warrigal spinach

— WARRIGAL SPINACH —

Warrigal spinach, New Zealand spinach, Botany Bay spinach, Warrigal greens or a wild spinach ground cover — lots of names but all the same nutritious plant — was used by Captain Cook as a tonic for scurvy. Cook's botanist, Sir Joseph Banks actually took spinach seeds back to England, where it is now grown as a summer green. Warrigal spinach is regarded as the first Australian food plant to be cultivated in Europe. This arrow-head shaped, green-leafed spinach is a common coastal vegetation, often seen near sandy areas and mangrove swamps. Like most leafy green vegetables, the spinach has many and varied uses. It can be seared and served with a main course of emu or kangaroo, or used in salads, roulades, pastry bases and soups.

Bush Spinach Soup

- *spinach leaves per person*
- *the same proportion of peeled potatoes*
- *dried onion flakes*
- *native peppercorns*
- *salt*
- *sufficient water to cover ingredients*

Method: Over hot coals, heat saucepan of water and blanch spinach for about three minutes. Discard water. Chop spinach.

Add about a litre of water to the clean saucepan, bring to boil and cook potatoes until they fall apart. Add spinach, peppercorns and salt. Gently mash potato and simmer for a further 20 minutes, making sure that there is always sufficient liquid.

WATTLE

A wattle is an acacia and is the background to Australia's Coat of Arms. Its yellow flowers form clusters and there are hundreds of different species. The wattle's seed is now the second commercialized native plant species on the market, following the macadamia nut. The seed is being harvested by Aborigines west of Australia's Great Dividing Range. Wattle seed has a nutty, coffee-like flavour and is high in protein.

Its versatility seems endless. Breads, cones, creams, pavlovas, ice creams, jellies, pancakes, blinis, sauces, chutneys, cakes, mousse and tea. If you are in the bush and have collected and roasted wattle seeds, brew yourself some wattle tea.

Wattle seeds

Wattle brewed in a saucepan

- 4 heaped teaspoons wattle seeds
- 1 roasting pan
- 1 medium saucepan ²/₃ full of water

Method: This is a fun way to make bush-made tea. Place saucepan of water on hot coals and heat. Place roasting pan alongside water saucepan and dry roast wattle seeds for a few minutes. Make sure that the seeds don't burn. Once roasted, tip into hot water saucepan and stir with a gum green stick. Even a little bit of the stick's gum flavour will alter, but not significantly, the tea's flavour. Bring tea to the boil, strain if possible and enjoy a healthy and rewarding cuppa with a few friends.

— WITCHETTY GRUBS —

A witchetty grub is actually a wood-boring, edible caterpillar of an Australian moth. It usually lays eggs in various species of wattle. The Aboriginal spelling of the witchetty is 'witjuti', which is the Arabana Aborigines word for two particular wattles.

When cooked so that the grub has a crispy skin and soft flesh, a witchetty grub is a taste sensation. Even better still, is the fact that most Australians are now learning that bush food includes more than witchetty grubs, fish and kangaroos. If you are wandering in the bush, remember that the grubs are borers and keep your eye out for old looking, witjuti bush. The grubs live in the underground roots and the soil will be cracked above its living quarters. Today witchetty grubs are not just roasted, but recipes range from cheese dip additives, to soup.

Witchetty Soup

- *10 fresh witchetty grubs*
- *40 ml oil*
- *dried onions*
- *1 litre stock*
- *2 chicken cubes*
- *native peppercorns*
- *salt*
- *½ pannikin (cup) powdered milk, made fairly thickly*
- *a little flour*

Method: This recipe serves about two people. In a saucepan sitting on hot coals, slowly saute grubs in oil. Add stock, crumbled cubes, dried onions, peppercorns and salt and cook for ½ hour. Add thickened milk. Add a little water to the flour and make into paste. Pour into soup and stir until it thickens slightly.

Joy Ross sampling a witchetty grub

YABBIES

Yabbies are prawn-like crustaceans and live in both fresh and salt-water.

There are several species of freshwater crayfish in Australia and the yabbie is one of them. It has the shape of a lobster, but the size of a king prawn. Its one large claw is larger on the male. A yabbie grows to about 15 cm and burrows in estuaries. After its hibernating period, it then emerges to spawn and shed its shell. Yabbies are found in sand, dams, lakes and creeks, particularly west of the Great Dividing Range and in South Australia.

If yabbies are caught in muddy streams, they need to be soaked overnight. In addition, when catching yabbies, it's best to keep them alive in water until they are cooked. Their flesh deteriorates very quickly when dead. Salt must be added to the water that yabbies are boiled in. You can tell when they are cooked, because their exo-skeletal shell turns orange/red.

Yabbie Cooking

Jack Absalom, well-known outback cook and television presenter, prefers this recipe for the simple cooking of yabbies.

Method: Bring a large container or water to the boil. Add salt in the ratio of $^3/_4$ kg salt to 18 litres water. Place the yabbies in the water and boil them for 3 minutes. Remove the pan from the heat and allow the yabbies to cool in the water. This will retain the moisture in the yabbies and give best results. When cool, drain and enjoy.

Yabbies Served on Gum Leaves

- 24 yabbies

Sauce
- 1 pint water
- 2 heaped tbls powdered milk
- 1 tbls flour
- 2 eggs
- salt and pepper to taste

Skewered yabbies

Yabbies on gum leaves

Method: Cook and clean yabbies, take off the tails and shell. Place yabbies in a pie dish or in camp oven. Now make the sauce. Put powdered milk and flour in a container and mix with a little cold water until you have a thickish mixture that will pour. Place saucepan on coals with the pint of water and bring to the boil. Remove from heat and add milk mixture stirring until nice and creamy. Now add the beaten egg, salt and pepper and stir well. Pour this in camp oven over yabbies. Heat through — cooking time is ½-1 hour. It seems sacrilege that yabbies are sometimes used for fishing bait; what a waste!

Skewered Yabbies

Many people carry smoked bacon in their packs. Apart from using it at breakfast with eggs, the flavours of yabbie and bacon make a great alternative taste.

- *24 large yabbie tails, shelled and washed*
- *6 bacon rashers*
- *Bamboo or metal skewers*

Method: Cut bacon in strips, half length wise. Wrap each yabbie tail in bacon, put on a skewer and grill over hot coals. Sometimes outback provisions include bush tomatoes, onions and fresh green vegetables. These can be successfully added to skewered yabbies and bacon. Cooking time: ten minutes.

ACKNOWLEDGEMENTS

The publishers gratefully thank the following for their photographic contribution to this title:

pages 13, 25 and 33: David Hancock/Skyscans
pages 17, 29 and 85: J. Brock/*Native Plants of Northern Australia*
pages 40, 41, 92 and 93: Jocelyn Burt/*Outback Cooking in the Camp Oven*
pages 45 and 89: Joy Ross
page 49: Patons Macadamia Plantations
pages 56, 69 and 81: Tim Low
page 68: Jennifer Isaacs
page 73: Tassal Limited
page 80: Tourism Tasmania